Jonas Brothers
Happiness Begins

PIANO
VOCAL
GUITAR

T0081431

ISBN 978-1-5400-6305-2

For all works contained herein:
Unauthorized copying, arranging, adapting, recording, Internet posting, public performance,
or other distribution of the music in this publication is an infringement of copyright.
Infringers are liable under the law.

Visit Hal Leonard Online at
www.halleonard.com

Contact us:
Hal Leonard
7777 West Bluemound Road
Milwaukee, WI 53213
Email: info@halleonard.com

In Europe, contact:
Hal Leonard Europe Limited
42 Wigmore Street
Marylebone, London, W1U 2RN
Email: info@halleonardeurope.com

In Australia, contact:
Hal Leonard Australia Pty. Ltd.
4 Lentara Court
Cheltenham, Victoria, 3192 Australia
Email: info@halleonard.com.au

SUCKER

Words and Music by NICK JONAS, JOSEPH JONAS,
MILES ALE, RYAN TEDDER, LOUIS BELL,
ADAM FEENEY and KEVIN JONAS

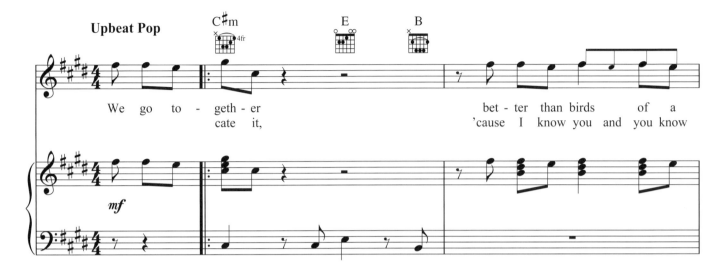

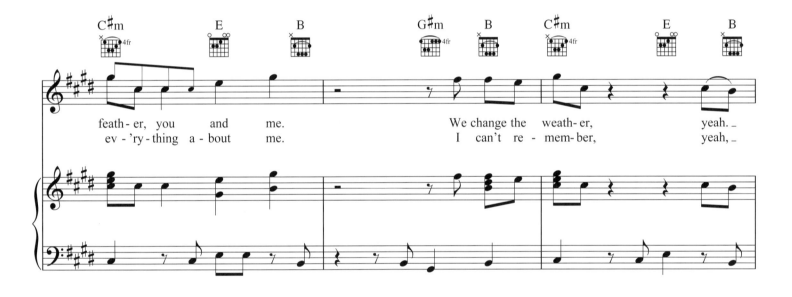

Copyright © 2019 SONGS OF UNIVERSAL, INC., NICK JONAS PUBLISHING, JOSEPH JONAS PUBLISHING, WRITE ME A SONG PUBLISHING,
EMI MUSIC PUBLISHING LTD., MYNY MUSIC, SAM FAM BEATS, EMI APRIL MUSIC INC. and KEVIN JONAS PUBLISHING DESIGNEE
All Rights for NICK JONAS PUBLISHING and JOSEPH JONAS PUBLISHING Administered by SONGS OF UNIVERSAL, INC.
All Rights for WRITE ME A SONG PUBLISHING Administered by DOWNTOWN MUSIC PUBLISHING LLC
All Rights for EMI MUSIC PUBLISHING LTD., MYNY MUSIC, SAM FAM BEATS and EMI APRIL MUSIC INC. Administered by
SONY/ATV MUSIC PUBLISHING LLC, 424 Church Street, Suite 1200, Nashville, TN 37219
All Rights Reserved   Used by Permission

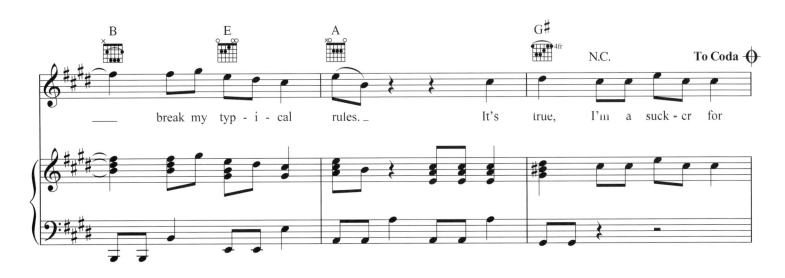

you,   yeah.   Don't com-pli -   you,   yeah.

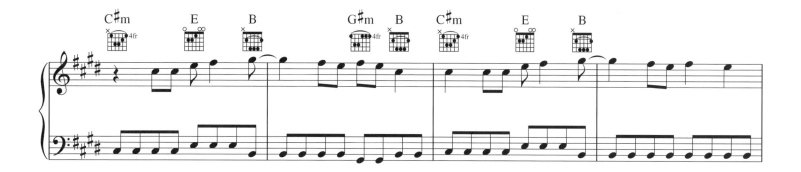

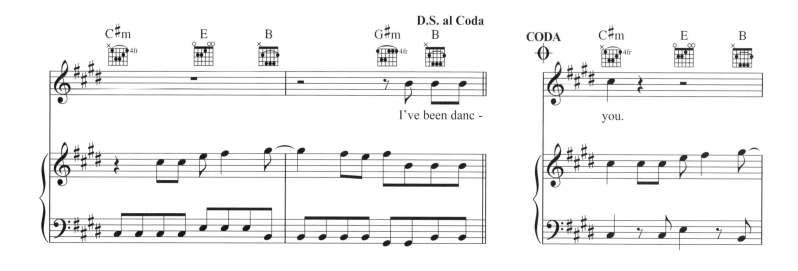

D.S. al Coda

CODA

I've been danc -   you.

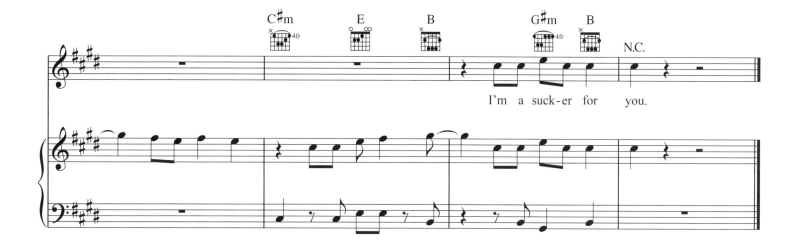

I'm a suck-er for   you.

COOL

Words and Music by NICK JONAS,
JOSEPH JONAS, KEVIN JONAS,
RYAN TEDDER, ZACH SKELTON
and CASEY SMITH

Moderate groove

I'm feel-ing so cool. From top to the bot-tom, just cool. Ev-'ry lit-tle thing that I

do. Damn it, I'm feel-ing so cool. _____ Yeah.

Woke up feel-ing like a new James Dean. I comb my hair like an old-school sheen.

Copyright © 2019 SONGS OF UNIVERSAL, INC., NICK JONAS PUBLISHING, JOSEPH JONAS PUBLISHING,
KEVIN JONAS PUBLISHING DESIGNEE, WRITE ME A SONG PUBLISHING and PATRIOT GAMES PUBLISHING
All Rights for NICK JONAS PUBLISHING and JOSEPH JONAS PUBLISHING Administered by SONGS OF UNIVERSAL, INC.
All Rights for WRITE ME A SONG PUBLISHING Administered by DOWNTOWN MUSIC PUBLISHING LLC
All Rights for PATRIOT GAMES PUBLISHING Administered by DOWNTOWN DLJ SONGS
All Rights Reserved   Used by Permission

And ev-'ry time that song comes on, it's a-bout ___ me. Oh, I feel like

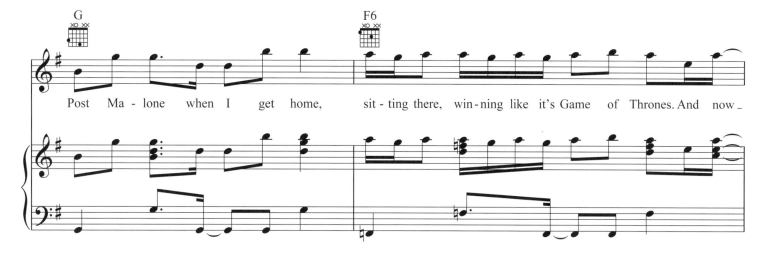

Post Ma - lone when I get home, sit - ting there, win-ning like it's Game of Thrones. And now ___

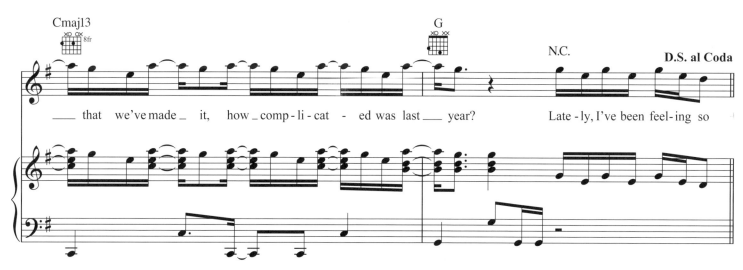

___ that we've made ___ it, how ___ comp - li - cat - ed was last ___ year? Late - ly, I've been feel-ing so

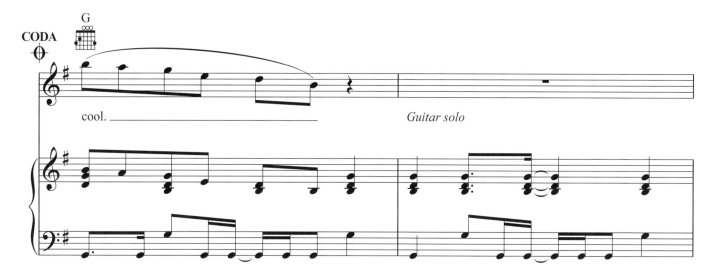

cool. _____ *Guitar solo*

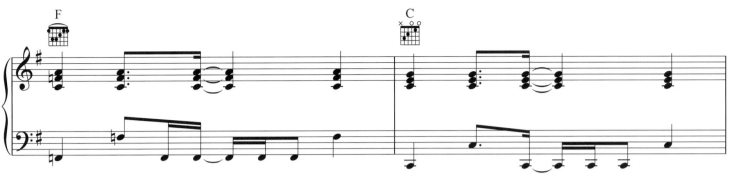

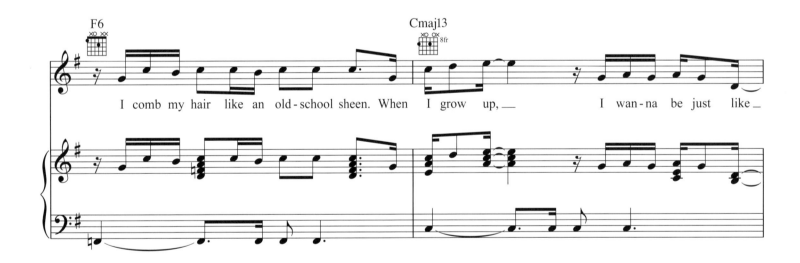

Solo ends   Woke up feel - ing like a new James Dean.

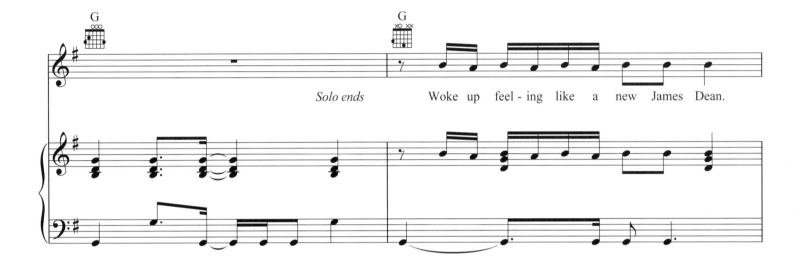

I comb my hair like an old - school sheen. When I grow up, ___ I wan - na be just like ___

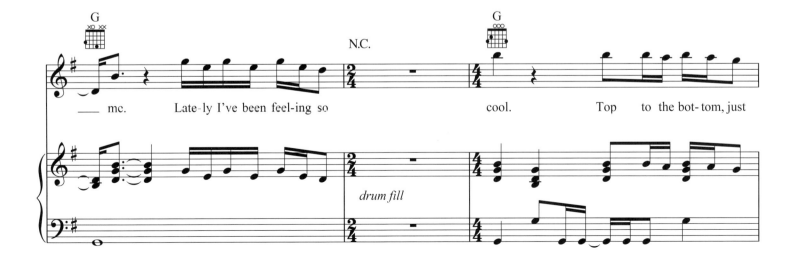

___ mc. Late - ly I've been feel - ing so   cool. Top to the bot - tom, just

drum fill

ONLY HUMAN

Words and Music by NICK JONAS,
JOSEPH JONAS, SHELLBACK
and KEVIN JONAS

Moderate Reggae

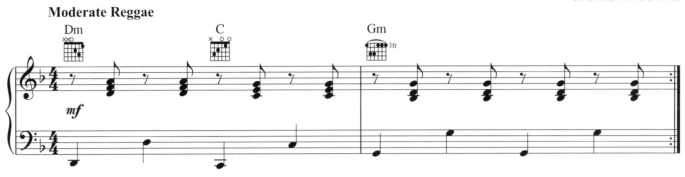

I don't want this night to end. ___ It's clos-

-in' time ___ so leave ___ with me ___ a - gain, ___ yeah. ___

Copyright © 2019 SONGS OF UNIVERSAL, INC., NICK JONAS PUBLISHING, JOSEPH JONAS PUBLISHING, MXM and KEVIN JONAS PUBLISHING DESIGNEE
All Rights for NICK JONAS PUBLISHING and JOSEPH JONAS PUBLISHING Administered by SONGS OF UNIVERSAL, INC.
All Rights for MXM Administered Worldwide by KOBALT SONGS MUSIC PUBLISHING
All Rights Reserved   Used by Permission

You got all my love to spend. _____ Oh, let's find _

___ a place _ where hap - pi - ness _ be - gins. _____ We gon'

dance in the liv - ing room, slave to the way you move. Hurts when I'm leav - in' you, ay. Just

dance in the liv - ing room, love with an at - ti - tude. Drunk to an eight - ies groove, _ ay. We gon'

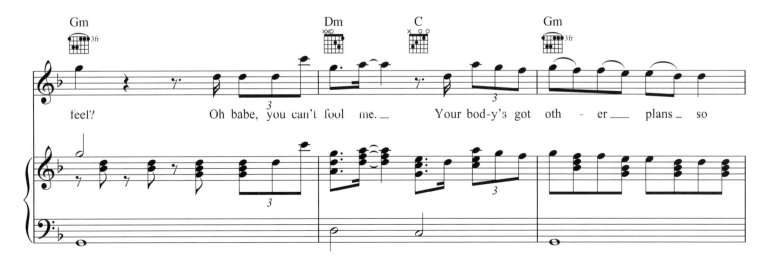

stop pre-tend-ing you're shy, just come on and dance, dance, dance, dance,

oh.

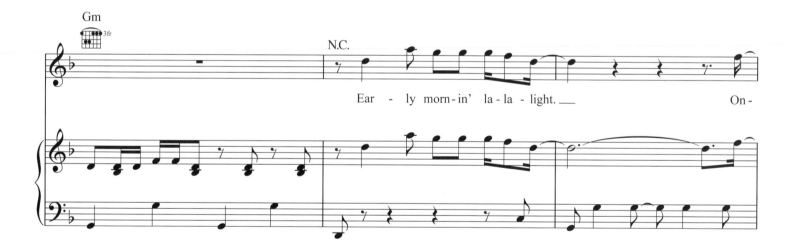

Ear - ly morn-in' la - la - light. On-

- ly get - tin' up to close the blinds. Oh,

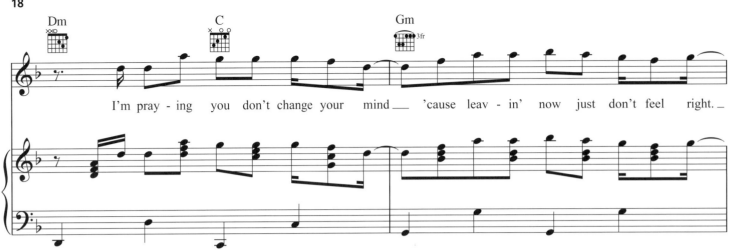

I'm pray - ing you don't change your mind __ 'cause leav - in' now just don't feel right. __

__ Let's do __ it one __ more time. _____ We gon'

D.S. al Coda

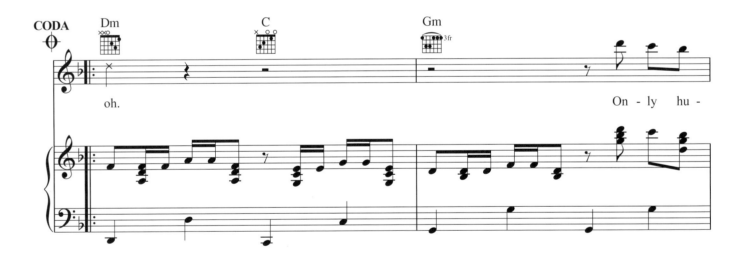

CODA

oh. On - ly hu -

man. It's on - ly man, it's on - ly man, on - ly hu - man.

I BELIEVE

Words and Music by NICK JONAS,
GREG KURSTIN and MAUREEN McDONALD

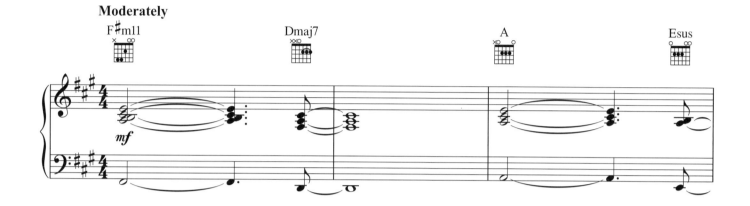

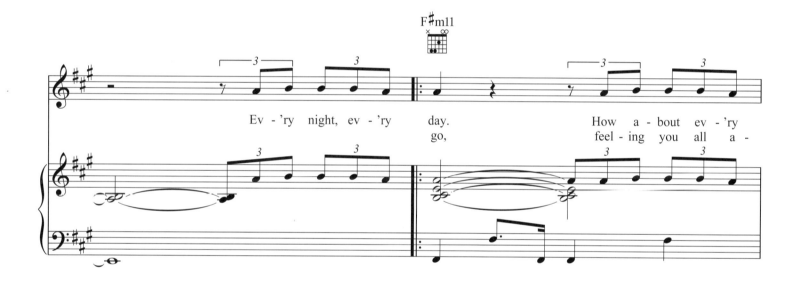

Ev - 'ry night, ev - 'ry   day.
go,

How a - bout ev - 'ry
feel - ing you all a -

life - time? ___   Yeah, I know what they   say,   and that's fine. ___
round   me. ___   Now that I've got you   close,   I'm al - right. ___

Copyright © 2019 SONGS OF UNIVERSAL, INC., NICK JONAS PUBLISHING,
EMI APRIL MUSIC INC., KURSTIN MUSIC and MO ZELLA MO MUSIC
All Rights for NICK JONAS PUBLISHING Administered by SONGS OF UNIVERSAL, INC.
All Rights for EMI APRIL MUSIC INC., KURSTIN MUSIC and MO ZELLA MO MUSIC Administered by
SONY/ATV MUSIC PUBLISHING LLC, 424 Church Street, Suite 1200, Nashville, TN 37219
All Rights Reserved   Used by Permission

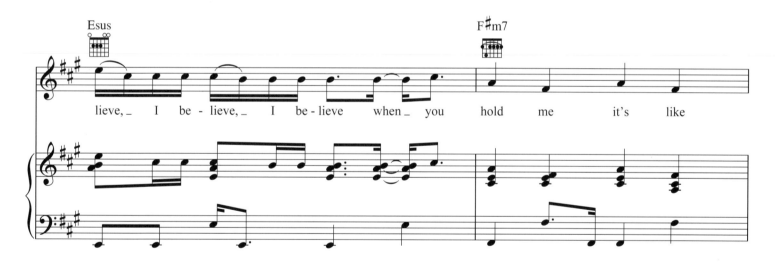

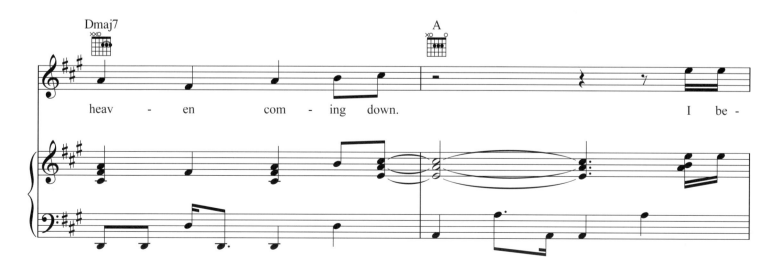

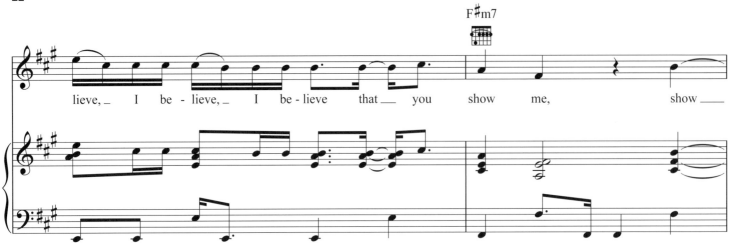

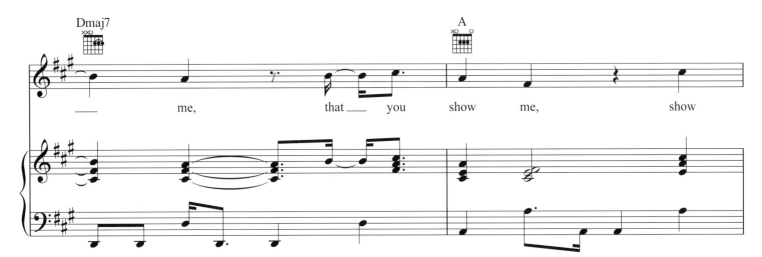

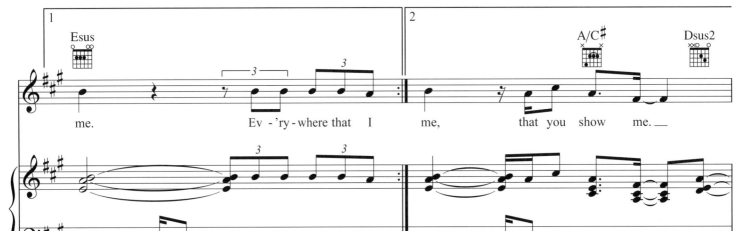

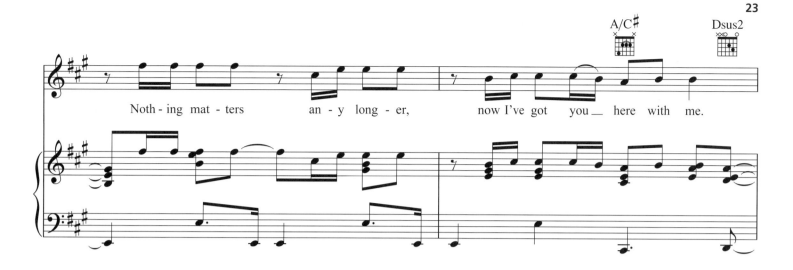

Noth-ing mat-ters an-y long-er, now I've got you___ here with me.

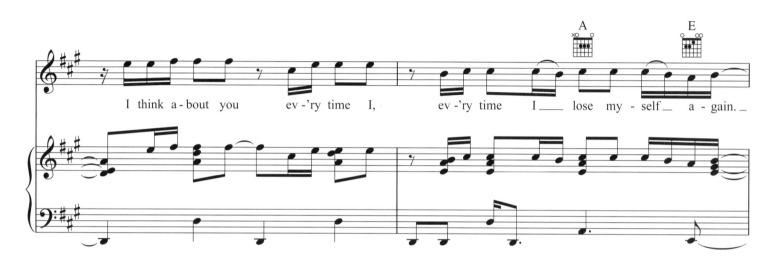

I think a-bout you ev-'ry time I, ev-'ry time I___ lose my-self___ a-gain.___

___ I lose my-self___ a-gain.___ 'Cause you

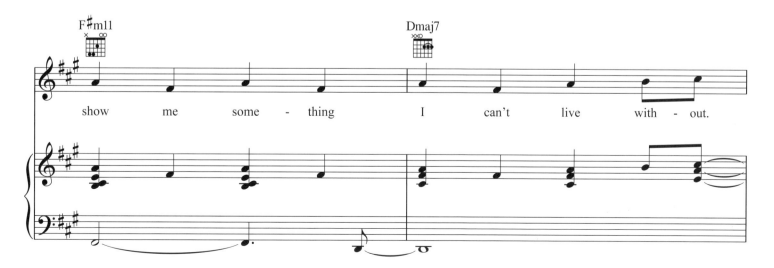

show me some-thing I can't live with-out.

I be - lieve,_ I be - lieve,_ I be - lieve when _ you

hold me it's like heav - en com - ing down.

I be - lieve,_ I be - lieve,_ I be - lieve 'cause you

show me some - thing I can't live with - out.   I bc -
(Lead vocal ad lib. on repeat.)

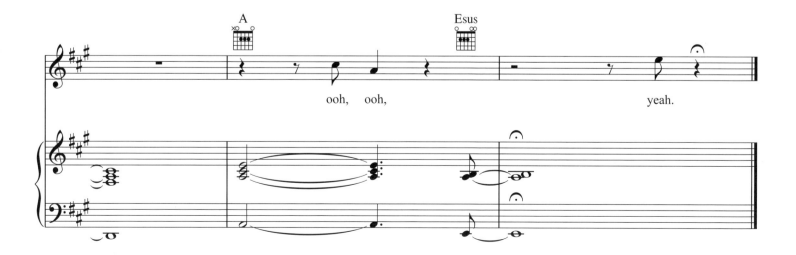

USED TO BE

Words and Music by NICK JONAS, JOSEPH JONAS,
LOUIS BELL, RYAN TEDDER, ZACH SKELTON
and KEVIN JONAS

* Recorded a half step lower.

Copyright © 2019 SONGS OF UNIVERSAL, INC., NICK JONAS PUBLISHING, JOSEPH JONAS PUBLISHING, LOUIS BELL PUBLISHING DESIGNEE
WRITE ME A SONG PUBLISHING, ALLIED ONE PUBLISHING, PATRIOT GAMES PUBLISHING and KEVIN JONAS PUBLISHING DESIGNEE
All Rights for NICK JONAS PUBLISHING and JOSEPH JONAS PUBLISHING Administered by SONGS OF UNIVERSAL, INC.
All Rights for WRITE ME A SONG PUBLISHING, ALLIED ONE PUBLISHING and PATRIOT GAMES PUBLISHING Administered by DOWNTOWN MUSIC PUBLISHING LLC
All Rights Reserved   Used by Permission

used to be the one I love. ___ Yeah, you used to be the one I, used to be the one ___ I. ___

Late - ly I don't ev - en know ya,   too man - y dev - ils on your shoul - der, shoul - der.
Woke up late ___ and I'm dream - in',   so tired of chas - in' all your de - mons, de - mons.

Oh my ___ God, ___ ba - by, is this what you ___ want? ___ Ooh, ___
Oh my ___ God, ___ ba - by, if it's what you ___ want. ___ Ooh, ___

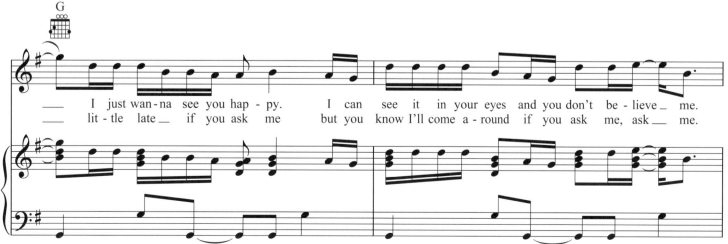

___ I just wan - na see you hap - py.   I can see it in your eyes and you don't be - lieve ___ me.
___ lit - tle late ___ if you ask me   but you know I'll come a - round if you ask me, ask ___ me.

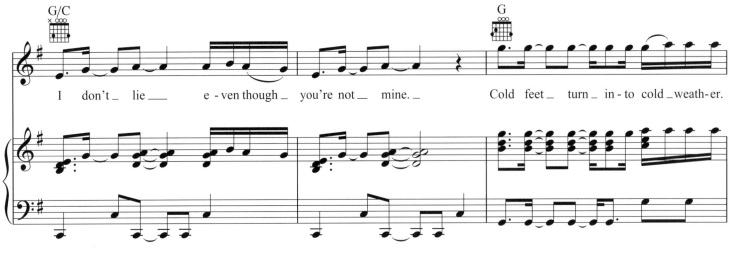

I don't lie __ e -ven though __ you're not __ mine. __ Cold feet __ turn __ in - to cold __ weath-er.

We had __ love, __ now it don't __ mat- ter. You just __ thought __ you could do __ bet- ter, so do __ bet- ter. __

Spend-in' all your time with your new friends and you take 'em all the plac- es now that we've been. But you

used to be the one I love. __ Yeah, you used to be the one I love. __

Say you wan-na talk, "How have you beens?" I'm the on-ly one you know that-'ll lis-ten and you

used to be the one I love. ___ Yeah, you used to be the one I loved, you used to be the

one. ___ Yeah, you used to be the one. _____ Yeah, you used to be the

one, _____ used to be the one. _____ Used to be the one ___ I. ___

EVERY SINGLE TIME

Words and Music by NICK JONAS,
JOSEPH JONAS, GREG KURSTIN
and MAUREEN McDONALD

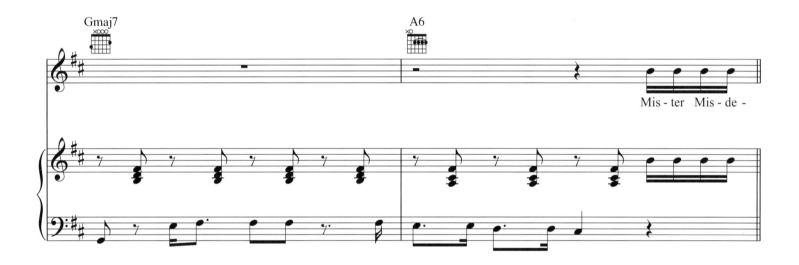

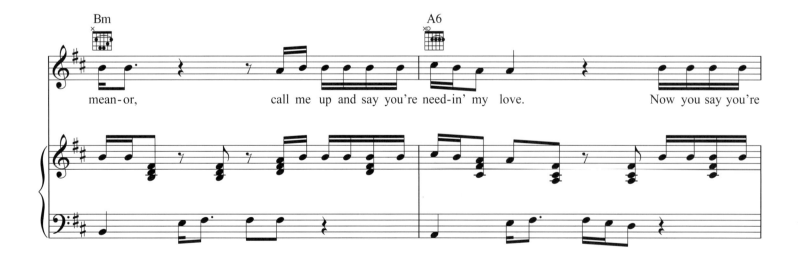

Copyright © 2019 SONGS OF UNIVERSAL, INC., NICK JONAS PUBLISHING, JOSEPH JONAS PUBLISHING, EMI APRIL MUSIC INC., KURSTIN MUSIC and MO ZELLA MO MUSIC
All Rights for EMI APRIL MUSIC INC., KURSTIN MUSIC and MO ZELLA MO MUSIC Administered by SONY/ATV MUSIC PUBLISHING LLC, 424 Church Street, Suite 1200, Nashville, TN 37219
All Rights Reserved   Used by Permission

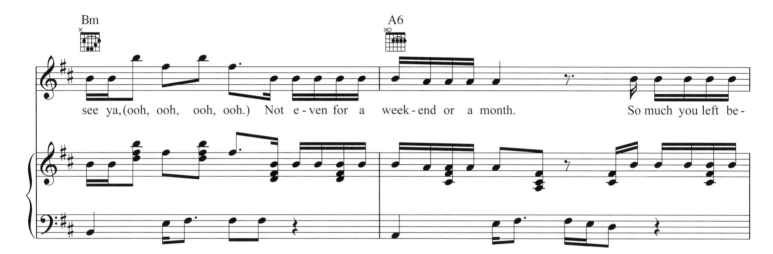

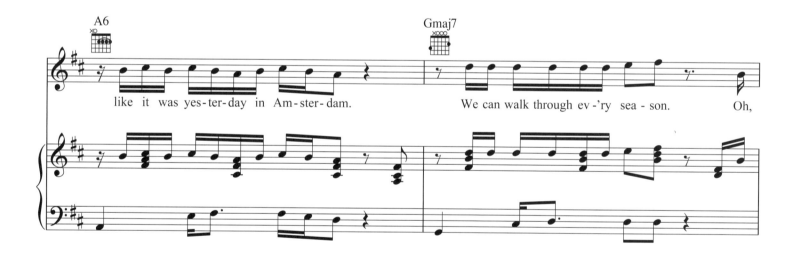

You think, you think it's on - ly phy - si - cal. No good at get - tin' e - ven the

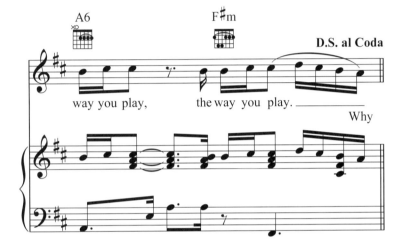

way you play, the way you play. Why

time, ime,

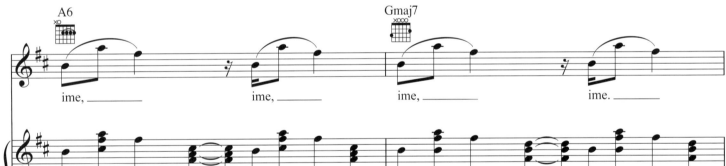

ime, ime, ime, ime.

Love locked down for you. Be - cause there's too much wa - ter un - der this bridge to go

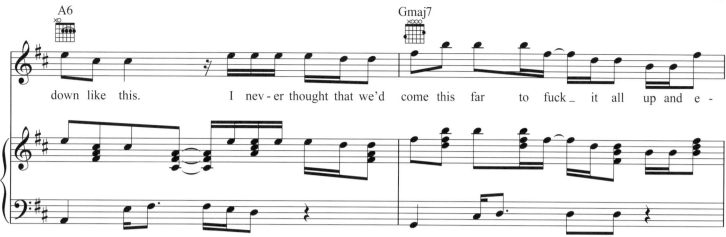

down like this. I nev-er thought that we'd come this far to fuck_ it all up and e -

end like this. Ev-'ry sin-gle time, I keep on com-in'

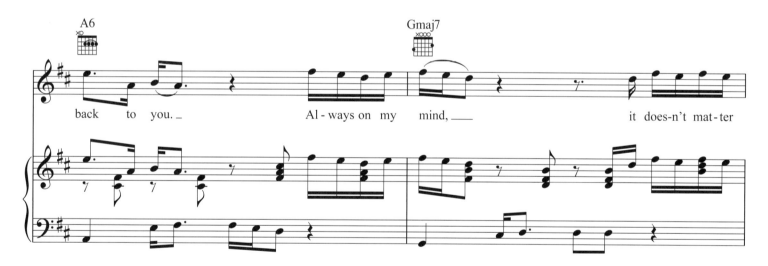

back to you._ Al-ways on my mind,___ it does-n't mat-ter

what I do._____ Ev-'ry sin-gle time,_____ I keep on com-in'

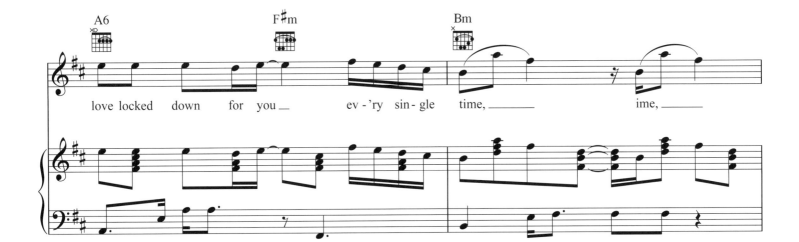

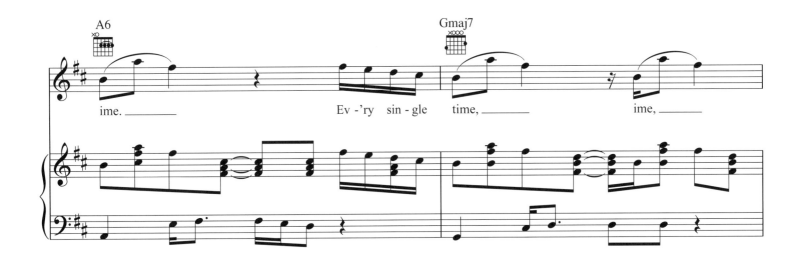

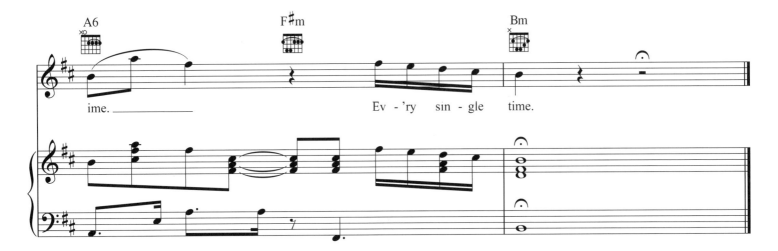

DON'T THROW IT AWAY

Words and Music by NICK JONAS, JOSEPH JONAS,
GREG KURSTIN and MAUREEN McDONALD

Moderate Pop

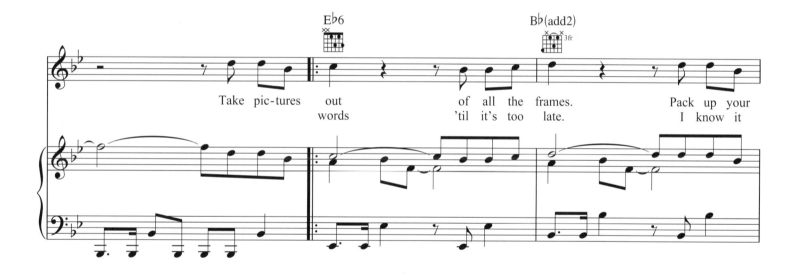

Take pic-tures out of all the frames. Pack up your
words 'til it's too late. I know it

love with all your things. See if it helps, give it a
hurts and that's o-kay. If it's too much to o-pen

Recorded a half step higher.

Copyright © 2019 SONGS OF UNIVERSAL, INC., NICK JONAS PUBLISHING, JOSEPH JONAS PUBLISHING, EMI APRIL MUSIC INC., KURSTIN MUSIC and MO ZELLA MO MUSIC
All Rights for NICK JONAS PUBLISHING and JOSEPH JONAS PUBLISHING Administered by SONGS OF UNIVERSAL, INC.
All Rights for EMI APRIL MUSIC INC., KURSTIN MUSIC and MO ZELLA MO MUSIC Administered by SONY/ATV MUSIC PUBLISHING LLC, 424 Church Street, Suite 1200, Nashville, TN 37219
All Rights Reserved   Used by Permission

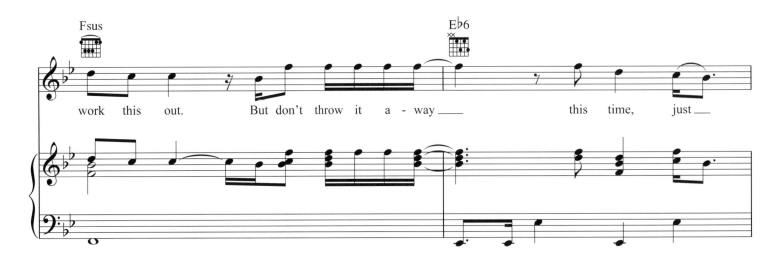

take a lit-tle time with me.__ Don't throw it a-way,__ it's fine, just__

don't for-get to think of me.__ Don't throw it a-way,__ your mind is__

mess-in' with your head a-gain.__ In-stead of walk-in' a-way,__ we should give it a break. Do it like I say,__

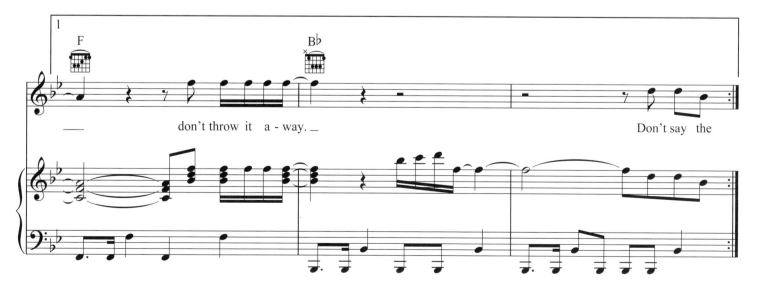

__ don't throw it a-way.__ Don't say the

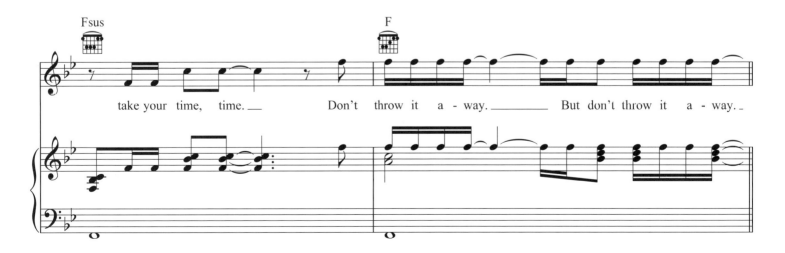

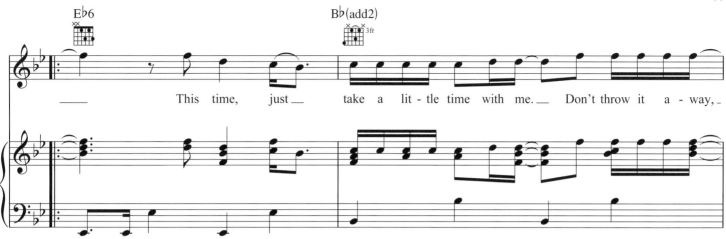

This time, just__ take a lit-tle time with me.__ Don't throw it a-way,__

it's fine, just__ don't for-get to think of me.__ Don't throw it a-way,__

your mind is__ mess-in' with your head a-gain.__ In-stead of walk-in' a-way,__

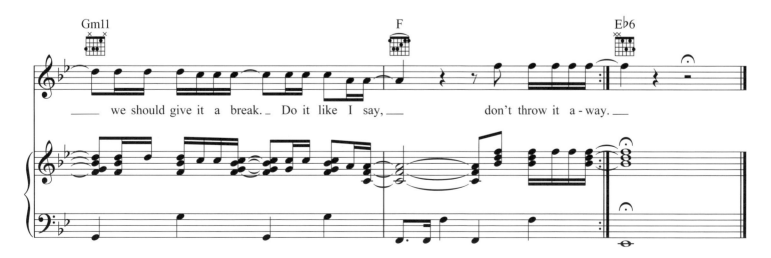

we should give it a break.__ Do it like I say,__ don't throw it a-way.__

LOVE HER

Words and Music by NICK JONAS,
JOSEPH JONAS and MIKE ELIZONDO

Acoustic Pop

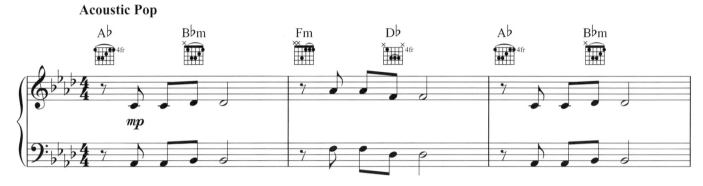

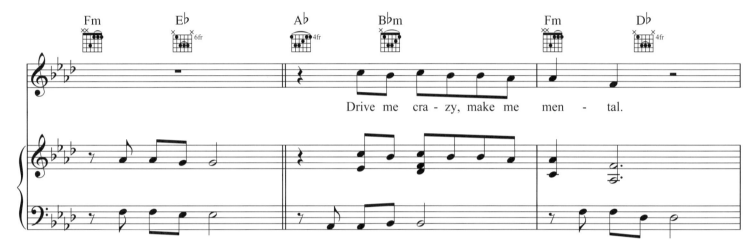

Drive me cra - zy, make me men - tal.

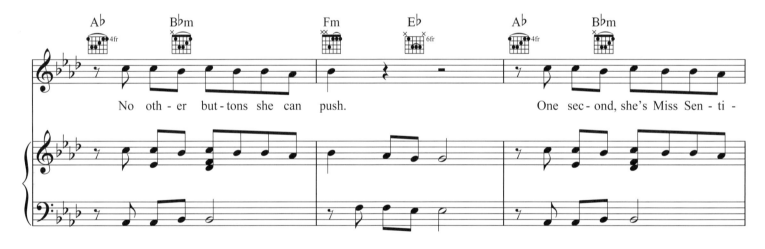

No oth - er but - tons she can push.

One sec - ond, she's Miss Sen - ti -

men - tal, then she's a - fraid she's said too much.

Copyright © 2019 SONGS OF UNIVERSAL, INC., NICK JONAS PUBLISHING, JOSEPH JONAS PUBLISHING and MIKE ELIZONDO PUBLISHING DESIGNEE
All Rights for NICK JONAS PUBLISHING and JOSEPH JONAS PUBLISHING Administered by SONGS OF UNIVERSAL, INC.
All Rights Reserved   Used by Permission

love her, la la la la la la love her, yeah.

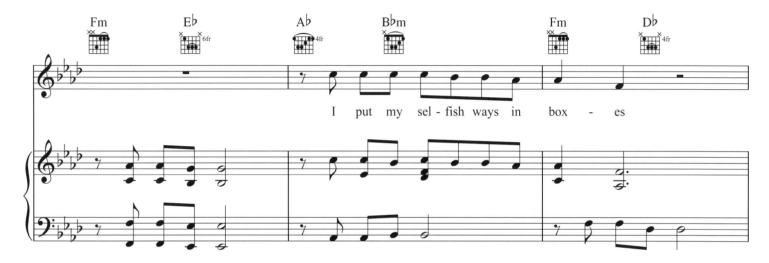

I put my sel-fish ways in box - es

and shipped them back to where they came. Will nev - er let it get close to be - ing

tox - ic and I prom - ise I'll nev - er walk a - way.

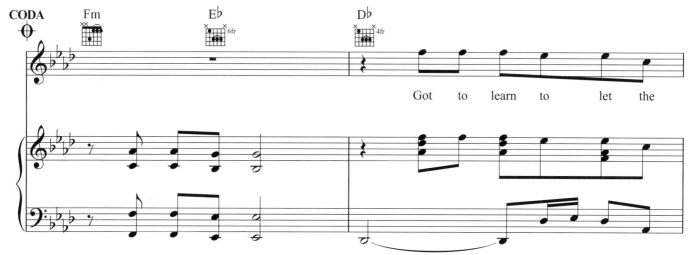

Got to learn to let the

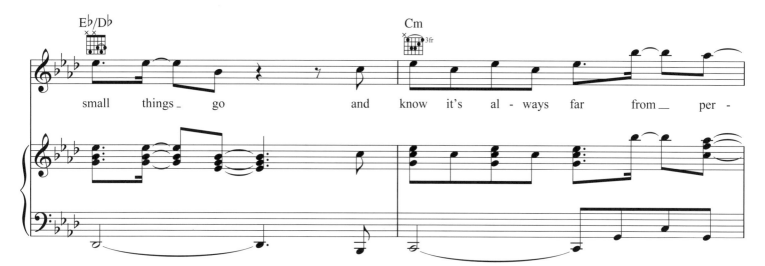

small things _ go and know it's al - ways far from _ per -

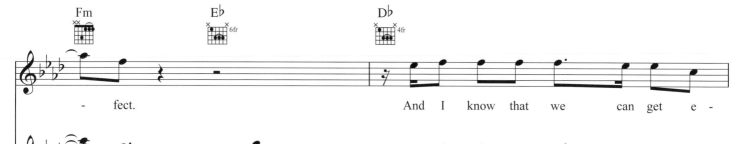

- fect. And I know that we can get e -

mo - tion - al, _____ but the hard - est parts are al - ways _ worth

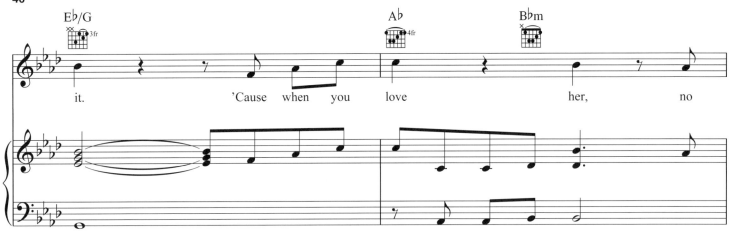

it. 'Cause when you love her, no

mat-ter the fight __ you know she's al-ways right, and that's al-right. And they say

love can hurt, ___ but see-ing her smile __ will get you ev-'ry time, yeah,

ev-'ry time. Be-cause you love her, la la la la ___ la la

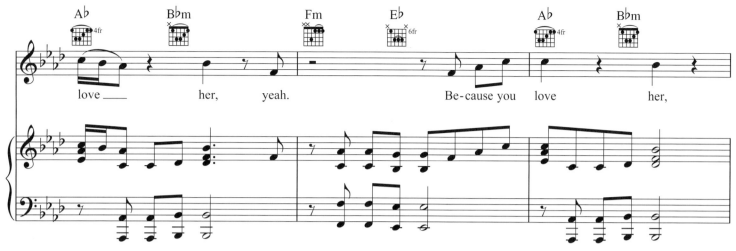

love _____ her, yeah. Be-cause you love her,

la la la la _____ la la la love her, yeah. Be-cause you,

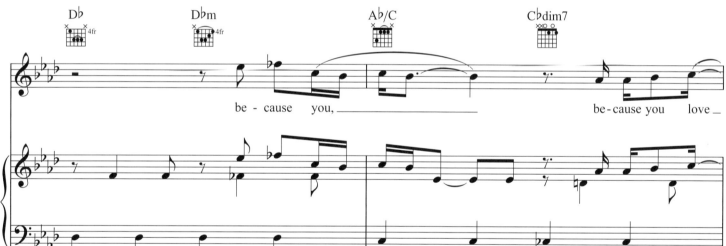

be - cause you, _____ be-cause you love _

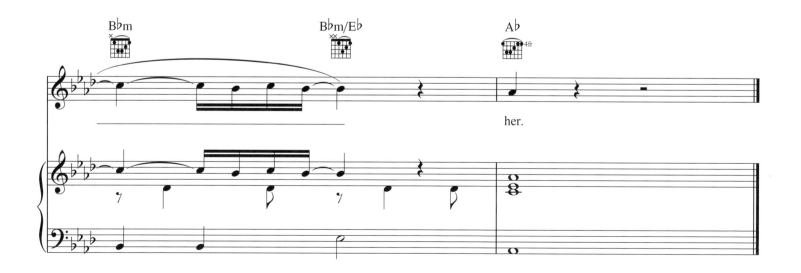

her.

HAPPY WHEN I'M SAD

Words and Music by NICK JONAS,
SARAH AARONS and JOEL LITTLE

Copyright © 2019 SONGS OF UNIVERSAL, INC., NICK JONAS PUBLISHING, EMI BLACKWOOD MUSIC INC.,
SONY/ATV MUSIC PUBLISHING (AUSTRALIA) PTY LTD. and EMI MUSIC PUBLISHING AUSTRALIA PTY LTD.
All Rights for NICK JONAS PUBLISHING Administered by SONGS OF UNIVERSAL, INC.
All Rights for EMI BLACKWOOD MUSIC INC., SONY/ATV MUSIC PUBLISHING (AUSTRALIA) PTY LTD. and EMI MUSIC PUBLISHING AUSTRALIA PTY LTD.
Administered by SONY/ATV MUSIC PUBLISHING LLC, 424 Church Street, Suite 1200, Nashville, TN 37219
All Rights Reserved   Used by Permission

They think I'm hap - py when I'm sad. They think I'm hap - py. They think I'm hap - py when I'm.

They think I'm hap - py. They think I'm hap - py when I'm sad. They think I'm hap - py.

They think I'm hap - py when I'm.
Hey, look how we

They think I'm hap - py when I'm. Nev - er gon - na stop,

nev - er gon - na calm down. Nev - er gon - na stop, they think I'm hap - py when I'm.

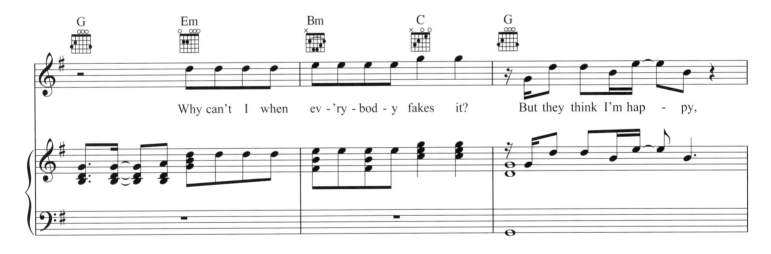

They think I'm hap - py when I'm sad. They think I'm hap - py. They think I'm hap - py when I'm.

They think I'm hap - py. They think I'm hap - py when I'm sad. They think I'm hap - py.

They think I'm hap - py when I'm. Nev-er gon - na stop, nev-er gon - na calm down.

Nev-er gon - na stop, they think I'm hap - py when I'm.

TRUST

Words and Music by NICK JONAS, JOSEPH JONAS,
RYAN TEDDER, JASON EVIGAN,
KEVIN JONAS and AMMAR MALIKE

Slow groove

I don't trust my-self ___ when I'm a-round you, ___ ooh. ___ I don't trust my-self ___ when I'm a-round you, ___ ooh. ___

Copyright © 2019 SONGS OF UNIVERSAL, INC., NICK JONAS PUBLISHING, JOSEPH JONAS PUBLISHING, WRITE ME A SONG PUBLISHING,
BMG PLATINUM SONGS US, BAD ROBOT, KEVIN JONAS PUBLISHNG DESIGNEE and MARU LA LA
All Rights for NICK JONAS PUBLISHING and JOSEPH JONAS PUBLISHING Administered by SONGS OF UNIVERSAL, INC.
All Rights for WRITE ME A SONG PUBLISHING Administered by DOWNTOWN MUSIC PUBLISHING LLC
All Rights for BMG PLATINUM SONGS US and BAD ROBOT Administered by BMG RIGHTS MANAGEMENT (US) LLC
All Rights for MARU LA LA Administered Worldwide by SONGS OF KOBALT MUSIC PUBLISHING
All Rights Reserved   Used by Permission

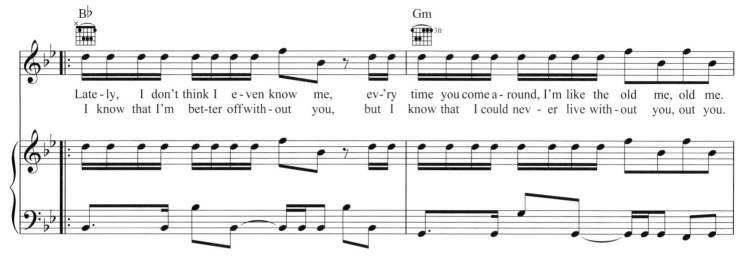

Late - ly, I don't think I e - ven know me, ev - 'ry time you come a - round, I'm like the old me, old me.
I know that I'm bet - ter off with - out you, but I know that I could nev - er live with - out you, out you.

Take me back to when you were my on - ly. We were thick - er than thieves, like a pod, two peas. } And
Think - ing 'bout my lips u - pon your mouth, yeah, got me weak at the knees, my _ God, can't breathe. } And

all at once _ it's like I'm be - ing some - one else. _ Yeah, you're

all I want _ but I know that you're bad for my health. _ I don't

you, _____ ooh. _____ I don't trust, I don't trust my - self. ___

I don't trust my - self, yeah. I don't trust, I don't trust my - self, ___

I don't trust my - self. I don't trust my - self ___ when I'm a - round

D.S. al Coda

CODA

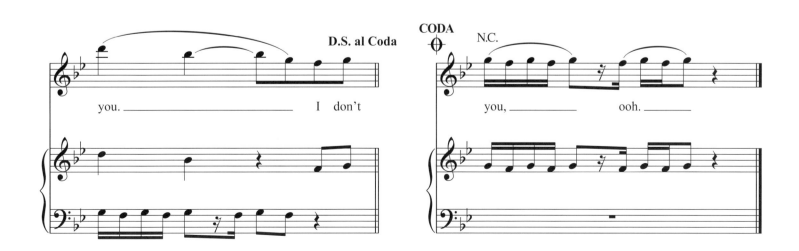

you. _____ I don't

N.C.

you, _____ ooh. _____

STRANGERS

Words and Music by NICK JONAS, JOSEPH JONAS,
GREG KURSTIN and MAUREEN McDONALD

Recorded a half-step higher

Copyright © 2019 SONGS OF UNIVERSAL, INC., NICK JONAS PUBLISHING, JOSEPH JONAS PUBLISHING, EMI APRIL MUSIC INC., KURSTIN MUSIC and MO ZELLA MO MUSIC
All Rights for NICK JONAS PUBLISHING and JOSEPH JONAS PUBLISHING Administered by SONGS OF UNIVERSAL, INC.
All Rights for EMI APRIL MUSIC INC., KURSTIN MUSIC and MO ZELLA MO MUSIC Administered by
SONY/ATV MUSIC PUBLISHING LLC, 424 Church Street, Suite 1200, Nashville, TN 37219
All Rights Reserved   Used by Permission

-'ry step back ___ pulls ___ me right back ___ to you.
___ me like that and pull ___ me right back ___ a - gain.

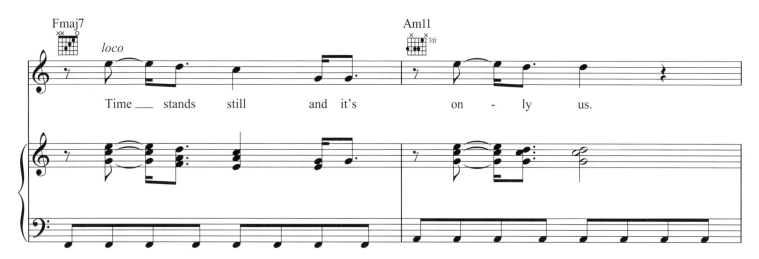

loco

Time ___ stands still and it's on - ly us.

What ___ we feel start - ed way be - fore we ev - er touched. ___

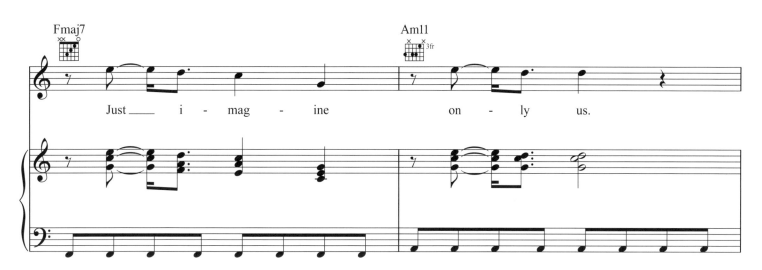

Just ___ i - mag - ine on - ly us.

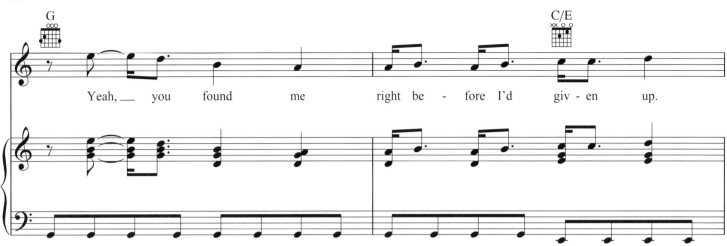

Yeah, __ you found me right be - fore I'd giv - en up.

I just saw __ the light - ning strike. Knew __ it right then when I

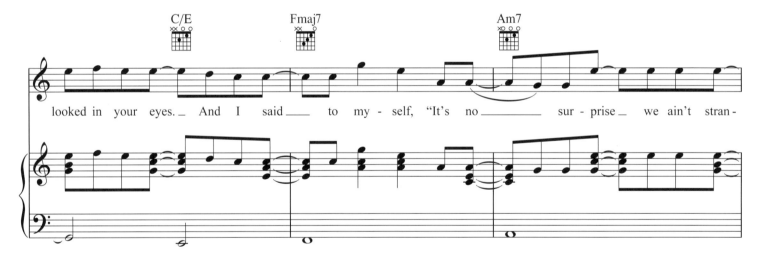

looked in your eyes. __ And I said __ to my - self, "It's no _____ sur - prise __ we ain't stran -

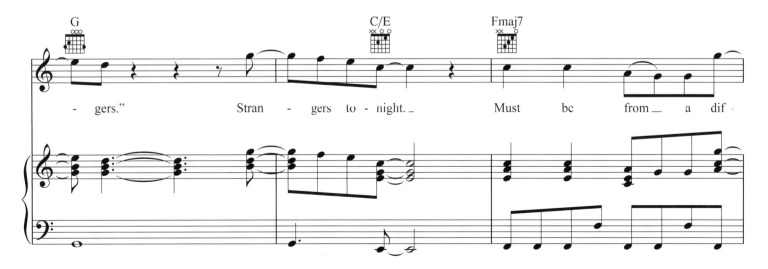

- gers." Stran - gers to - night. __ Must be from __ a dif -

-f'rent life, been ___ here be - fore ___ and it just ___ feels ___ right. ___ No, this ain't ___

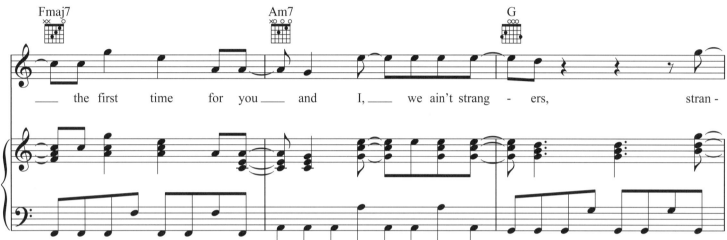

___ the first time for you ___ and I, ___ we ain't strang - ers, stran -

- gers to - night. ___ Stran - gers. Stran -

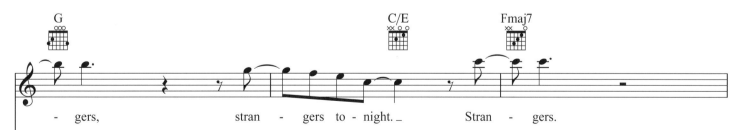

- gers, stran - gers to - night. ___ Stran - gers.

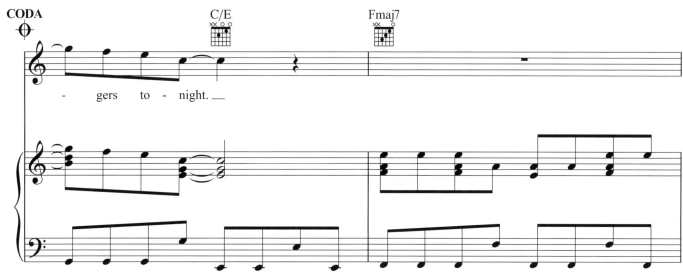

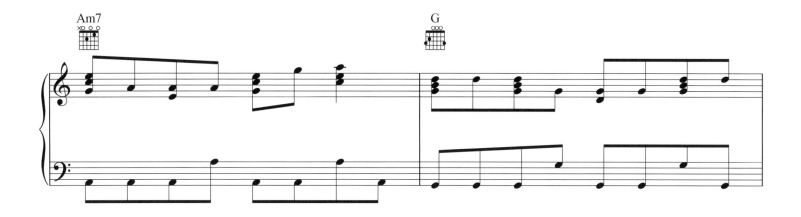

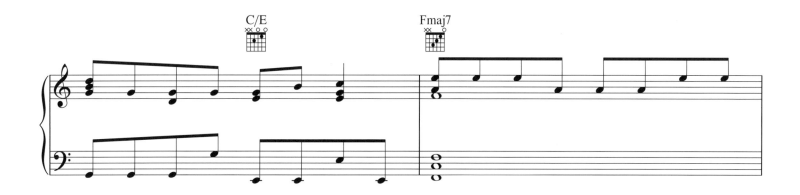

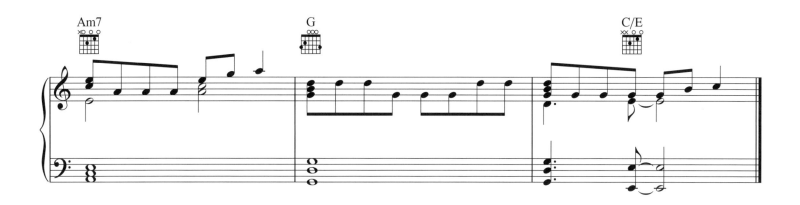

HESITATE

Words and Music by JOSEPH JONAS,
KENNEDI LYKKEN, JUSTIN TRANTER
and MIKE SABATH

Kiss the tears right off your face. ___
Don't you ev - er say good - bye. ___

Won't get scared, that's the old, old, old ___ me.
Cross my heart and you can keep, keep, keep ___ mine.

I'll be there, time and
If I could on - ly read your

Copyright © 2019 JOSEPH JONAS PUBLISHING, WARNER-TAMERLANE PUBLISHING CORP., KENNEDI LYKKEN PUBLISHING DESIGNEE,
MARQUISE CAT PUBLISHING, JUSTIN'S SCHOOL FOR GIRLS and MIKE SABATH PUBLISHING DESIGNEE
All Rights for JOSEPH JONAS PUBLISHING Administered by SONGS OF UNIVERSAL, INC.
All Rights for KENNEDI LYKKEN PUBLISHING DESIGNEE, MARQUISE CAT PUBLISHING and
JUSTIN'S SCHOOL FOR GIRLS Administered by WARNER-TAMERLANE PUBLISHING CORP.
All Rights Reserved   Used by Permission

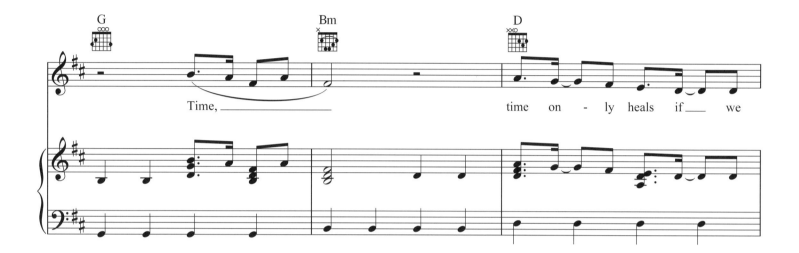

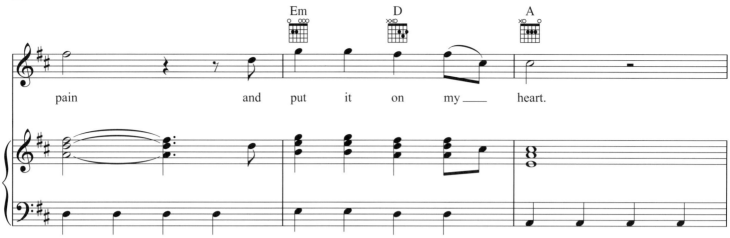

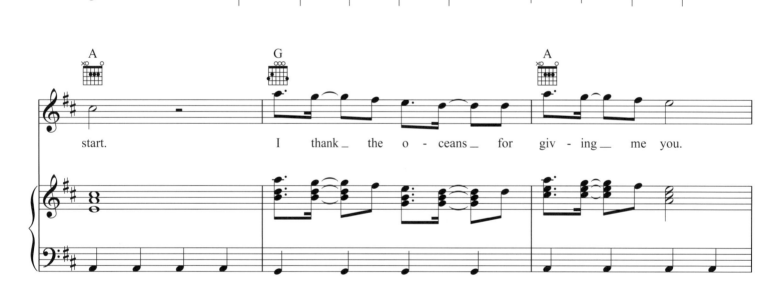

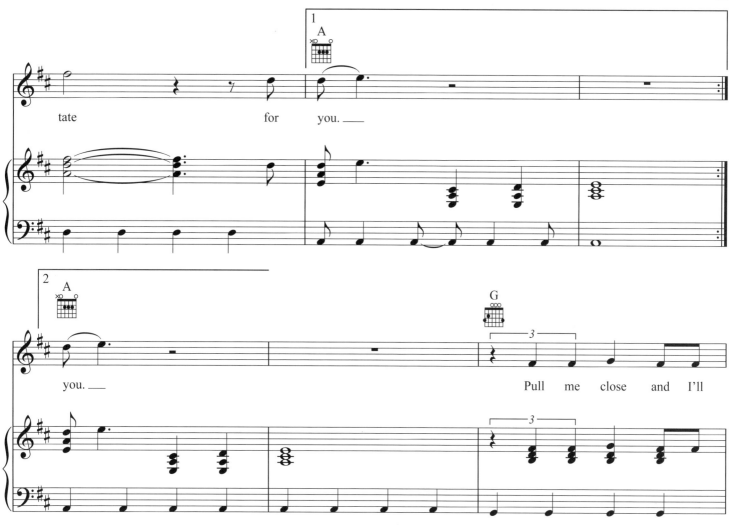

tate   for   you. ___

you. ___   Pull   me   close   and   I'll

hold __ you tight. __   Don't be scared __ 'cause I'm on __ your side. __

Know there's noth - in' I would - n't do __ for   you. _____

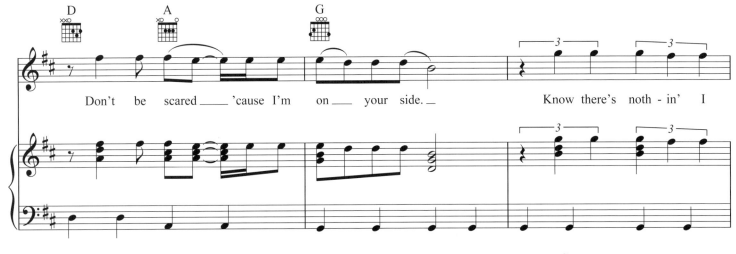

Pull me close and I'll hold you tight.

Don't be scared 'cause I'm on your side. Know there's noth-in' I

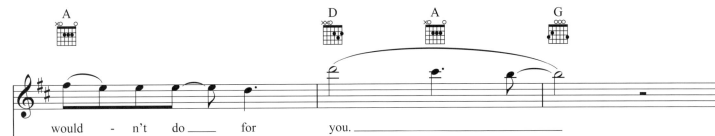

would-n't do for you.

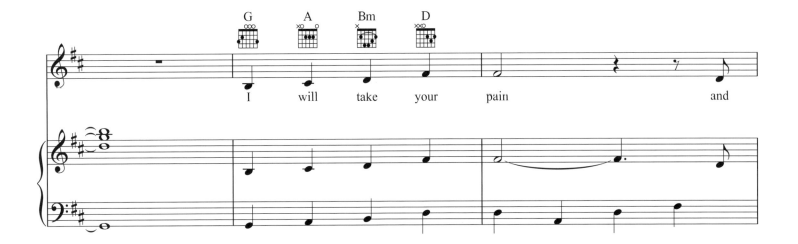

I will take your pain and

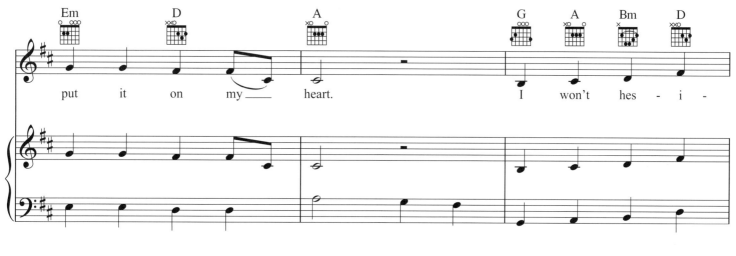

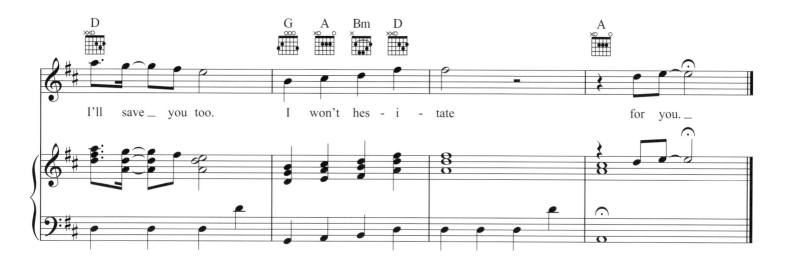

ROLLERCOASTER

Words and Music by ZACHARY SKELTON,
RYAN TEDDER, CASEY SMITH, MICHAEL POLLACK
and JONAS JEBERG

Laid-back Pop

Nights fly - ing down the ten, near - ly two __ A.
Faith led me to the clouds, reach - ing for __ the

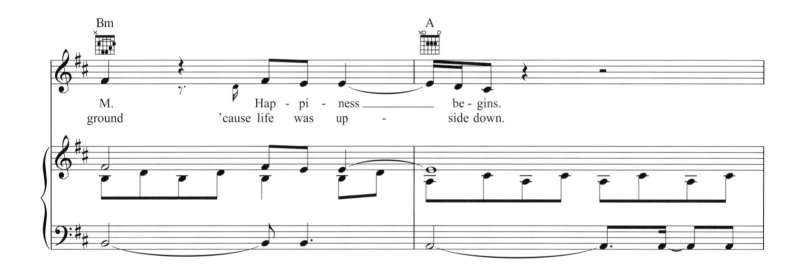

M. Hap - pi - ness __ be - gins.
ground 'cause life was up - side down.

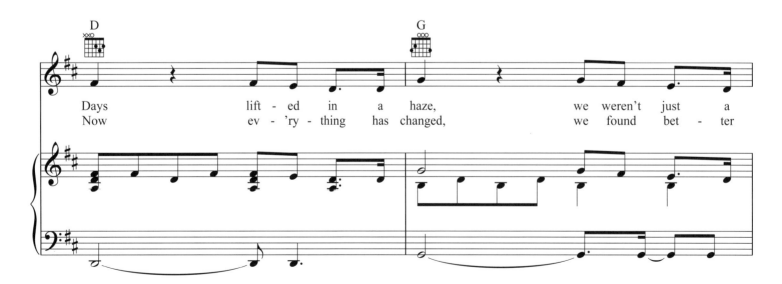

Days lift - ed in a haze, we weren't just a
Now ev - 'ry - thing has changed, we found bet - ter

Copyright © 2019 Allied One Publishing, Fourteen Hands, Patriot Games Publishing, Warner-Tamerlane Publishing Corp.,
What Key Do You Want It In Music, Songs With A Pure Tone and Jonas Jeberg Publishing Designee
All Rights for Allied One Publishing, Fourteen Hands and Patriot Games Publishing Administered by Downtown Music Publishing LLC
All Rights for What Key Do You Want It In Music and Songs With A Pure Tone Administered by Warner-Tamerlane Publishing Corp.
All Rights Reserved   Used by Permission

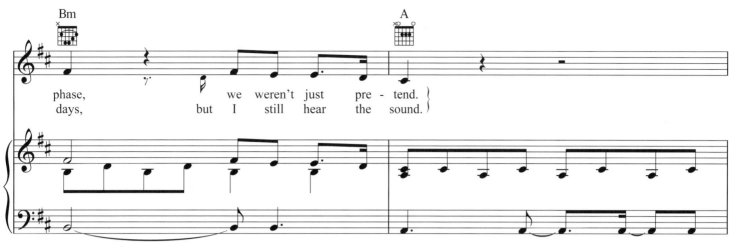

phase,   we weren't just pre - tend.
days,   but I still hear the sound.

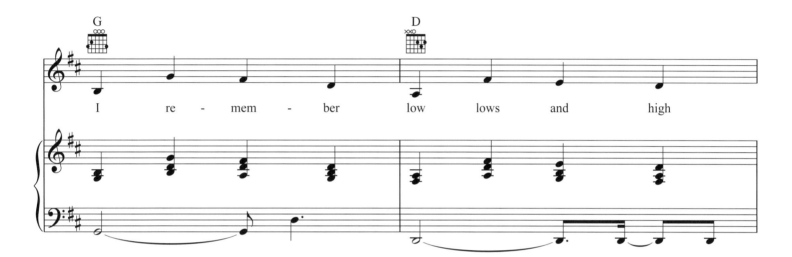

I re - mem - ber low lows and high

highs. _____

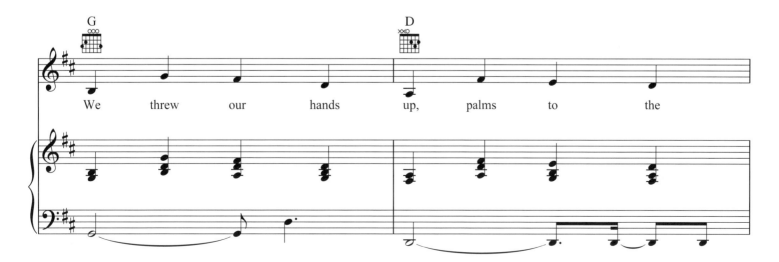

We threw our hands up, palms to the

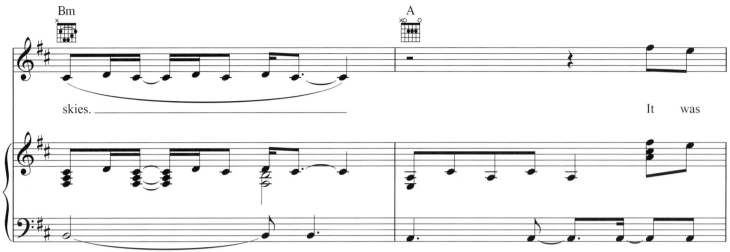

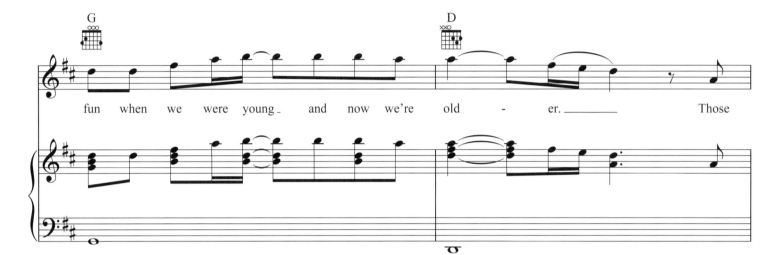

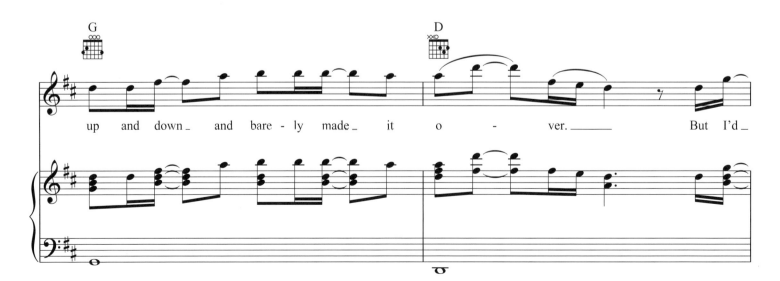

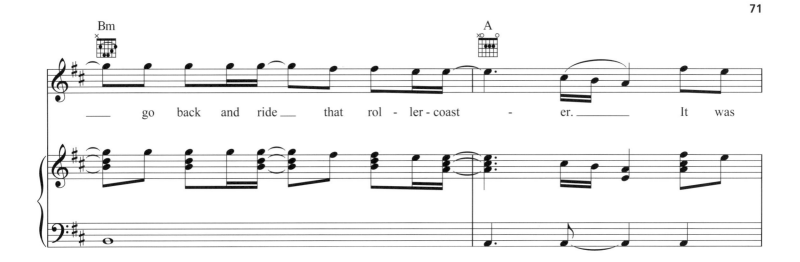

go back and ride __ that rol - ler - coast - er __ with you.

Ooh. ____

Ooh. ____

Ooh. ____ But I'd __

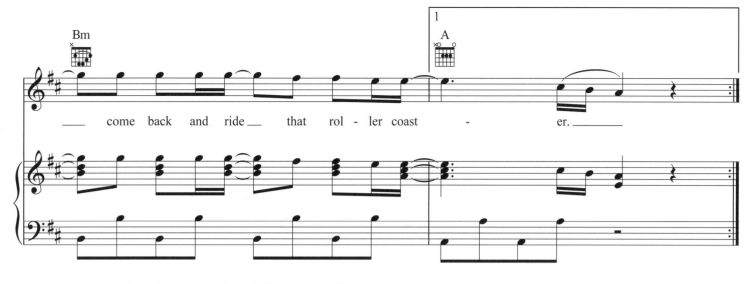

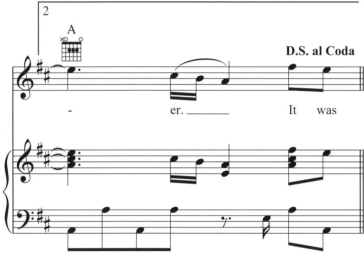
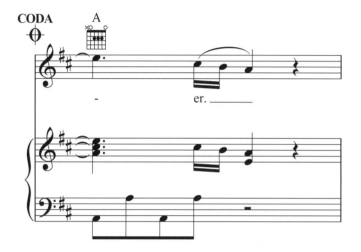

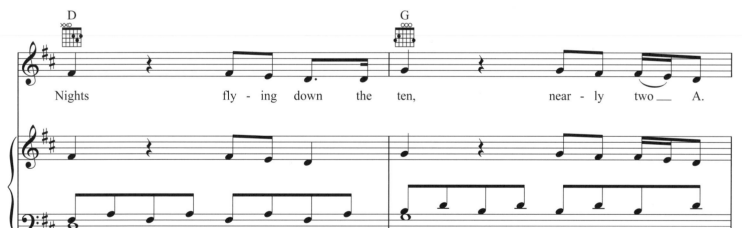

COMEBACK

Words and Music by NICK JONAS, JOSEPH JONAS,
SYLVESTER WILLY SIVERTSEN, JAMES ALAN GHALEB
and KEVIN JONAS

Copyright © 2019 SONGS OF UNIVERSAL, INC., NICK JONAS PUBLISHING, JOSEPH JONAS PUBLISHING,
TIGERSPRING SONGS, MARTIN SHADOWSKI MUSIC GROUP, ANNAMYLOVE MUSIC, MXM and KEVIN JONAS PUBLISHING DESIGNEE
All Rights for NICK JONAS PUBLISHING, JOSEPH JONAS PUBLISHING and TIGERSPRING SONGS Administered by SONGS OF UNIVERSAL, INC.
All Rights for MARTIN SHADOWSKI MUSIC GROUP, ANNAMYLOVE MUSIC and MXM Administered Worldwide by SONGS OF KOBALT MUSIC PUBLISHING
All Rights Reserved   Used by Permission

are right now, know some-how I'll be on the way like a bat out-ta hell. Heav-en

knows I'm proud but I'll turn 'round. Ba - by, if you stay then I won't let you down. oh. ____

____ What - ev - er we've_ done, what - ev - er we'll_ do. Ba - by, if you

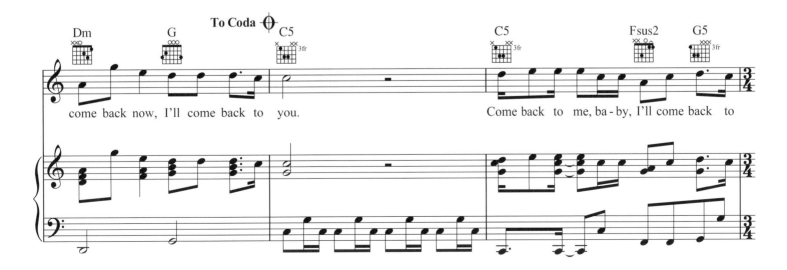

come back now, I'll come back to you. Come back to me, ba - by, I'll come back to

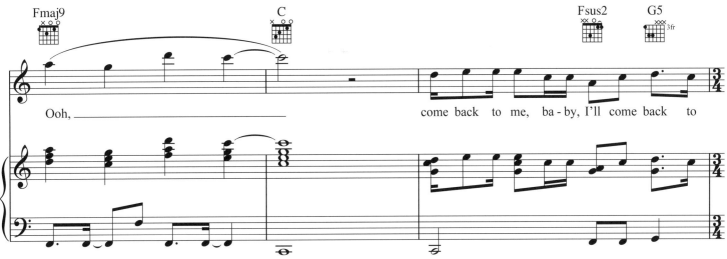

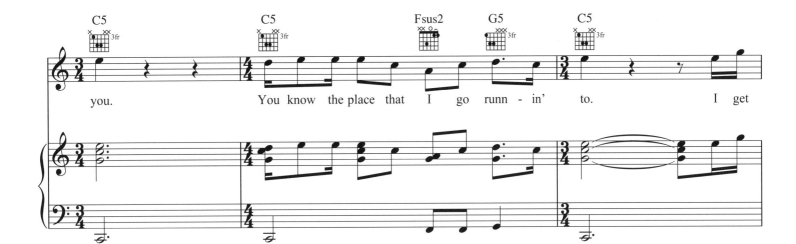

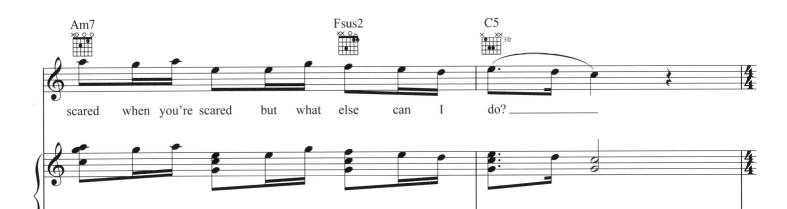

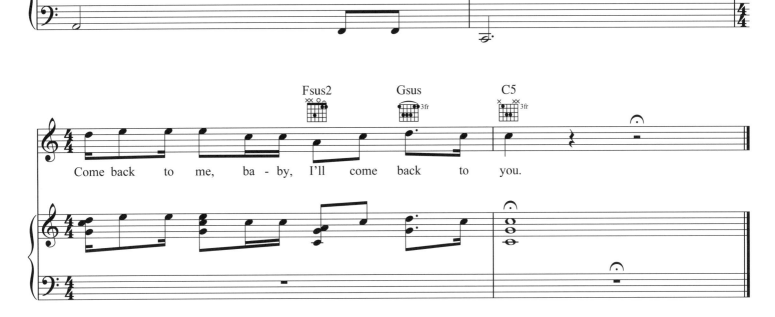